DATE DUE			
APR 05 2014	MAR 0 5 2019		
JUL 15 2014			
SEP 3 0 2014			
OCT 0 8 2014			
MAR 2 5 2015			
JAN 2 7 2016			
OCT 1 7 2017			
JAN 2 6 2018			
OCT 1 1 2018			

Modern Rhymes About Ancient Times

ANCIENT EGYPT

Written by Susan Altman and Susan Lechner

Illustrated by Sandy Appleoff

Children's Press®
A Division of Scholastic Inc.
New York • Toronto • London • Auckland • Sydney
Mexico City • New Delhi • Hong Kong
Danbury, Connecticut

THE SPHINX, THE PYRAMIDS,
The odd hieroglyphic;
Mystery medicines,
Books scientific;
Mummies and pharaohs,
From long-ago times.
You'll learn about all of them
Reading these rhymes.

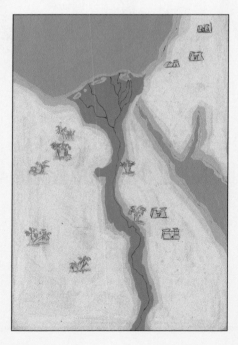

With much love to Eve—who combines the best of Hatshepsut and Nefertiti.—S. R. A.

To Jennifer and Michael, whose willingness to be challenged can begin here—with love.—S. L.

Reading Consultant: Nanci Vargus, Ed.D., Decatur Township Schools, Indianapolis, Indiana

Book production by Editorial Directions, Inc.

Book design by Marie O'Neill

Library of Congress Cataloging-in-Publication Data
Altman, Susan.
    Ancient Egypt / written by Susan Altman and Susan Lechner ; illustrated by Sandy Appleoff.
    p. cm. — (Modern rhymes about ancient times)
    Includes bibliographical references and index.
    ISBN 0-516-21149-8 (lib. bdg.)   0-516-27372-8 (pbk.)
    1. Egypt—History—To 640 A.D.—Juvenile poetry. 2. History, Ancient—Juvenile poetry. 3. Children's poetry, American. [1. Egypt—Civilization—To 332 B.C.—Poetry. 2. American poetry.] I. Lechner, Susan. II. Appleoff, Sandy, ill. III. Title. IV. Series.
    PS3551.L7943 A84 2001
    811'.54—dc21   2001028200

TABLE OF CONTENTS

SPHINX

It sits there silent in the sand,
Created by an unknown hand,
Swathed in sculpted mystery,
Time turns into history.
The mighty Sphinx,
Carved mass of stone,
Waiting, watching,
All alone.
What do you know?
What have you seen?
Of pharaohs passing with their queens,
Of caravans with silk and gold,
On route to fabled cities, old.
Of battles lost,

And battles won,
As time unfolds beneath the sun.
Who carved your face?
Who traced your eye?
And set you there
Against the sky?
The mighty Sphinx,
Carved mass of stone,
Waiting, watching,
Sits alone,
Gazing into history,
Holding fast to mystery,
With majestic dignity,
Silent through eternity.

The Sphinx is more than 4,000 years old. Its body is 240 feet (73 meters) long. Each of its eyes is 6 feet (2 meters) high.

PYRAMIDS

How did they build the pyramids
Without bulldozers, forklifts, or cranes?
How did they move those mountains of stone?
The mystery boggles our brains.

How did they build the pyramids?
What were the methods they used?
Who plotted the angles? Who figured things out?
The experts are still quite confused.

Erected as tombs for pharaohs of old,
These wonderful structures still stand.
Created 5,000 years in the past,
Their secrets are lost in the sand.

PPER EGYPT, LOWER EGYPT

Upper Egypt, Lower Egypt,
Yes, it is perplexing,
'Cause Lower's up and Upper's down.
It's really very vexing.

The River Nile flows South to North
(For those of you just setting forth),
So check the maps right in your books,
Down-river's *up*—or so it looks!

And if you travel *up* the Nile,
That's *upper* Egypt, mile by mile.
But on a map, you're heading *down*.
No wonder students wear a frown.

Upper Egypt, Lower Egypt,
Some think it's amusing
That Lower's *up* and Upper's *down*.
To me it's just confusing.

PHARAOHS

Emperors, rulers, tyrants, and kings.
The pharaohs of Egypt were all of these things.

Arrayed in fine jewels, gold bracelets, and silk,
They ordered great statues and pyramids built.
They sent forth their armies with banners unfurled,
Made Egypt respected all over the world.

Emperors, rulers, tyrants, and kings.
The pharaohs of Egypt were all of these things.

Rulers supreme, lords of the land,
From the Nile's muddy waters to Sahara's hot sand.
Divided by dynasty, centuries old,
The whole of their story has never been told.

Pharaoh is pronounced FAIR-oh.

THE PHARAOH MENES (About 3200 B.C.)

He brought together North and South.

Of him, this much is known.

He unified all Egypt

And sat upon its throne.

Menes is pronounced MEE-neez.

11

MUMMIES

In Egypt, when a pharaoh died,
They didn't use formaldehyde.*
Instead, they used a secret way
To keep his body from decay.
They checked him out from head to toes
And pulled his brain out through his
   nose.
Then dipped him in their special sauce,
And wrapped him up in strips of gauze,
And placed him in a pyramid
With lots of food, then closed the lid.
Said if you opened up his tomb,
You'd face a scary, endless doom.

Today, in movies, mummies scare
All those who are not yet aware,
Who fear an ancient mummy's curse
Could turn you green—and maybe
   worse.
But mummies really aren't bad.
It's just they're bored and maybe sad.
For many years, they lay just so,
All wrapped up—no place to go.

*Formaldehyde's a kind of juice
That keeps dead frogs for future use
By someone, like a scientist,
Who wants to know why frogs exist.

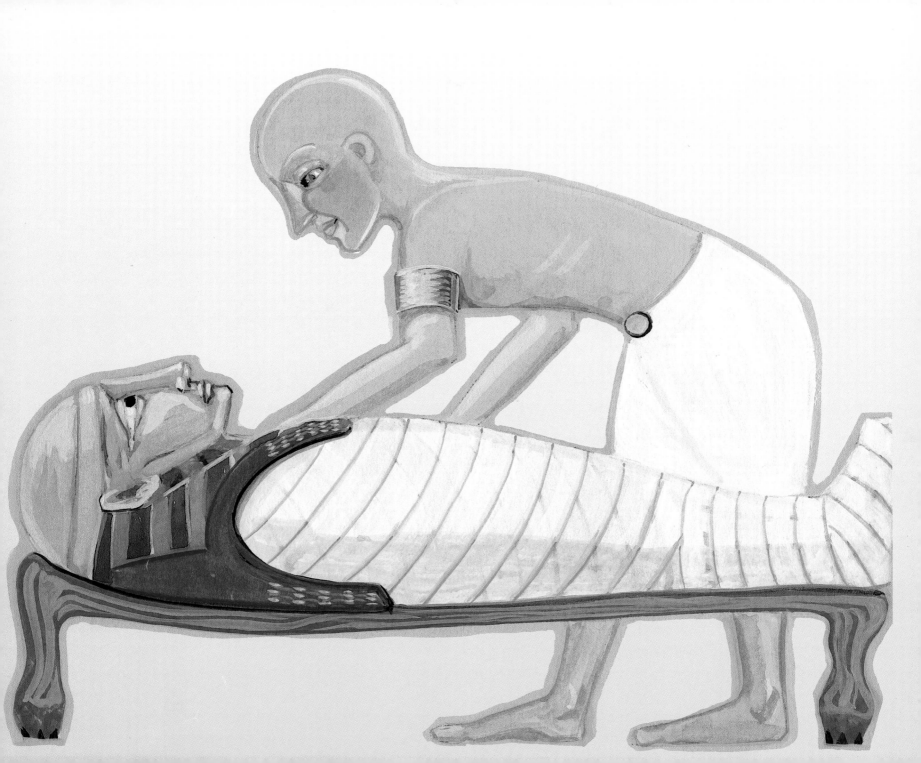

IEROGLYPHICS

Egyptians had no A-B-C;
They didn't read like you and me.
Instead they made up hieroglyphics.
Every picture was quite specific.

This is a foot, and
This is a hand.
What does this mean— ?
It's the sign for a queen.

A horse; a mouth;
An owl; a cat
A loaf; a snake;
A gate; a mat.

Sometimes the pictures were all in a line,
Sometimes on top of each other.
And using different symbols was perfectly fine—
Here is just one sign for "mother."

Each symbol presented a challenge—
How to place it, and face it, and space it.
After all, when you're carving in stone,
There's just no easy way to erase it.

Hieroglyphics is pronounced high-row-GLIFF-ix.

PAPYRUS

You could use it as a fuel.
You could put it in your soup.
You could weave it into sandals
Or a lovely chicken coop.
You could make it into boxes.
You could twist it into twine.
The plant they called papyrus
Was so versatile and fine.
You could make it into sailboats.
You could braid it into cloth,
And you never had to worry
About damage by a moth.
But the best thing 'bout papyrus
As you'll all agree, I think—

You could use it just like paper.
All you needed was the ink.
You flattened out the stems,
Laid them all out side by side,
And then another layer of
Papyrus was applied.
Sprinkle water from the Nile.
Add some nice papyrus juice
To keep it stuck together
So that nothing could come loose.
Writing on papyrus
Was much easier than clay,
And the only thing you had to do
Was know just what to say.

SCRIBES

Since most Egyptians couldn't read
And fewer still could write.
You'd think that they would then be in
A rather sorry plight.

How to keep their records?
Send letters to their kin?
Write their laws and contracts?
That's where the scribes came in.

Trained from early childhood,
Their classes were quite tough.
Young scribes were beaten often
To make them learn their stuff.

But once their trade was mastered
And they wielded brush and pen,
They also wielded power—
Scribes were most important men.

Today we have computers
To keep our records straight.
Back then, the scribes did all the work.
In fact, they ran the state.

# ROSETTA STONE

For many years through history,
Egypt was a mystery.
'Cause nobody could read specifics
Of ancient Egypt's hieroglyphics.

Then Jean-François Champollion
Asked soldiers of Napoleon
To let him study what they'd found—
A big rock lying on the ground.

Marked in Greek and hieroglyphic,
It turned out to be terrific.
It gave Champollion the key
To unlock all that mystery.

Named for the place where it was found,
The Rosetta stone is world renowned.

SCARABS

The scarab is a bug.
Ugh!

They make little balls from the earth.
In Egypt, this stood for rebirth.

Craftsmen carved scarabs from stone,
And silver and gold—even bone.

They served as a magical charm
To keep you from evil and harm.

Priests removed brains from the dead
And put in a scarab instead.

We marvel today at this fuss,
Since the scarab
    means nothing to us,

Just a bug.
Ugh!

HYKSOS

Almost 4,000 years ago
From Asia, fast they came.
Standing in horse-drawn chariots,
The Hyksos rode to fame.

They conquered Egypt and Syria.
They ruled for one hundred years.
Defeated at Tanis, they vanished forever,
Lost in history's tears.

Hyksos is pronounced HIK-sos.

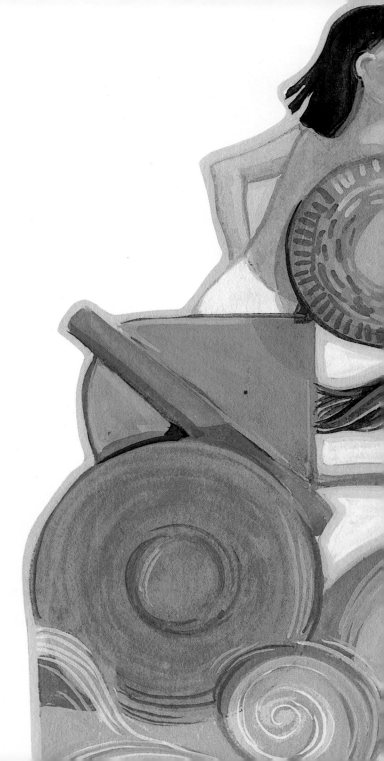

ISIS

In a crisis,
Call on Isis,
Goddess of all life.
She's the sister
Of Osiris.
(She also is his wife.)

Often pictured
Wearing cow horns
Underneath the sun.
In a crisis,
Call on Isis.
She is number one.

Isis is pronounced EYE-siss.
Osiris is pronounced oh-SYE-russ.

 ECO

The Pharaoh Neco wanted to be all that he could be,
So he ordered a canal built from the Nile down to the sea.
Unfortunately, it didn't work; the ditch filled up with sand.
But Neco had the right idea; his plan was rather grand.

There weren't many maps back then, and those they
    had were poor,
But Neco wanted answers; he wanted to be sure.
Just how big was Africa? What was its size and shape?
Where was there an inlet? Where was there a cape?
He hired Phoenician sailors, noted for their skill.
They sailed around the continent; Neco paid the bill.

The Pharaoh Neco wanted to be all that he could be,
And his geographic efforts have gone down in history.

Phoenician is pronounced fuh-NEE-shun. *Neco* is pronounced NEK-oh.

HE NILE RIVER

The Nile was the center of all life in ancient Egypt.
On its shores the famous cities known as Thebes and Luxor lay.
Most people lived beside the river's gently flowing waters,
    And it's still like that today.

Although Egypt is a country where the land is mostly desert,
By the river, crops would grow and land was fertile for a while.
Farmers harvested their cotton, and their date trees, and their wheat fields,
    On the land beside the Nile.

Once a year the river flooded; this was not a cause for sadness.
Farmers waited for the time the Nile would overflow its banks.
The river brought new life to fields that needed irrigation
    And Egyptians gave their thanks.

KARNAK AND LUXOR

Now, if you visit Egypt,
To Karnak you must go
To see great Amun's temple,
Where worshipers bowed low.

There you'll see the columns,
Arranged in sixteen rows,
And walk along the shrines and halls
Built there so long ago.

Not far away is Luxor,
Another famous site,
With statues, halls and obelisks,
And temples to delight.

So if you visit Egypt,
You'll view the ruins with zest..
At Luxor and at Karnak
You'll get to see the best.

Karnak is pronounced CAR-nack. *Luxor* is pronounced LUX-or. *Amun* is pronounced AH-mun.

AMUN

Amun was chief god of Egypt,
He and wife, Mut, were divine.
Though he had a ram's head,
It's always been said
That he managed to have a good time.

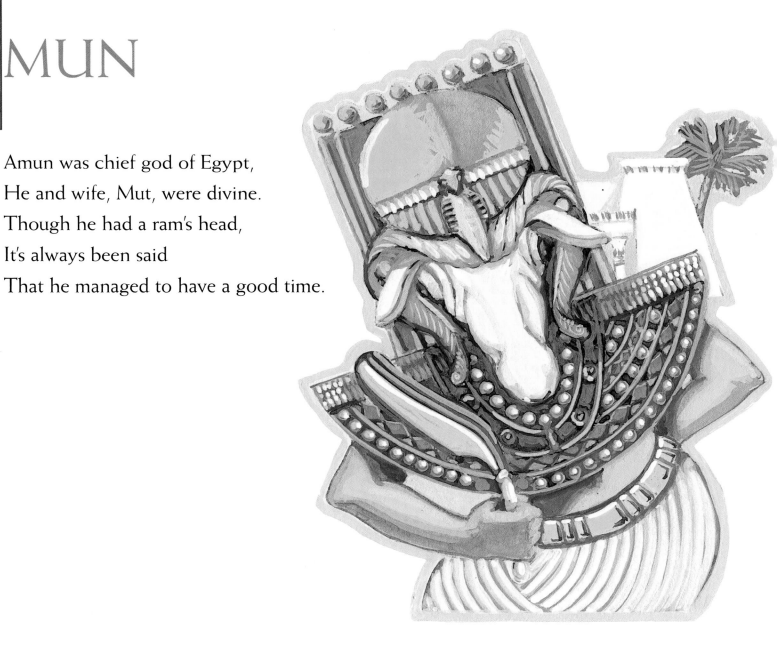

# HATSHEPSUT (15th century B.C.)

Hatshepsut, female pharaoh, liked to wear a beard.
She said it was important to be sure that she was feared.
Although her stepson, Thutmose, was supposed to rule the land,
Hatshepsut soon took over and ruled as she had planned.

She brought Egyptians years of peace, expanded foreign trade,
And built a lavish temple where her statues were displayed.
But Thutmose was quite jealous, and when Queen
    Hatshepsut died,
He had those statues broken up to soothe his injured pride.

The word "Hatshepsut" looks hard,
But there's no need to take fright.
Take a breath, close your eyes, and just say,
"Hat-SHEP-soot," and you will be right!

Thutmose is pronounced TUT-moze.

# NEFERTITI (Early 14th century B.C.)

Nefertiti, Nefertiti,
Beautiful Egyptian queen.
Nefertiti, Nefertiti,
Calm and lovely, all serene.
Nefertiti, Nefertiti,
Were you brave or smart or kind?
We remember just your beauty,
All the rest is left behind.

Nefertiti is pronounced NEF-er-TEE-tee.

KING TUT (14th century B.C.)

In 1922,
In the Valley of the Kings,
They found his tomb still hidden,
And filled with wondrous things.
Inside a golden casket
With jewels in rich display,
The boy-king Tutankhamen
In silent splendor lay.
His face behind a golden mask,
Gold scepter in his hand,
Golden bowls and daggers,
The world at his command.

He died so young, a teenage boy,
A name inside a story,
Remembered now forever
In all his regal glory.

His name was Tutankhamen,
But folks call him King Tut.
'Cause Tutankhamen's just too long
To say without a cut.

Tutankhamen is pronounced TOOT-in-COMMON.

AMSES II (13th century B.C.)

Ramses was a pharaoh,
Held in high esteem.
He conquered all his enemies
So he could rule supreme.

He raised up mighty monuments
That told of all his deeds
And built a massive pyramid
For his eternal needs.

And then he met with Moses, who
Said, "Let my people go."
But Ramses was too mean and proud,
And he told Moses, "No."

Well, Moses called upon the Lord
To make the king relent.
It took a lot of doing
Before Ramses would consent.

Ramses was a pharaoh.
Ramses was supreme.
He made all Egypt tremble
During his regime.

NCIENT EGYPTIAN DOCTORS

Some skills were known
Like setting a bone

Or stitching a cut,
BUT

Egyptians had treatments quite hard to endure,
But patients were happy when there was a cure.

If a child were quite ill, growing weaker and thin,
They fed him a mouse (first removing its skin).

For a pain in the head, the treatment they tried
Was rubbing the spot with a fish, lightly fried.

Hippopotamus poop was a favorite cure,
Though just how it worked, they were never
    quite sure.

But mostly the doctors would call on their gods
And cast magic spells to help even the odds.

They struggled to combat disease and decay,
But frankly I'm glad they can't treat me today.

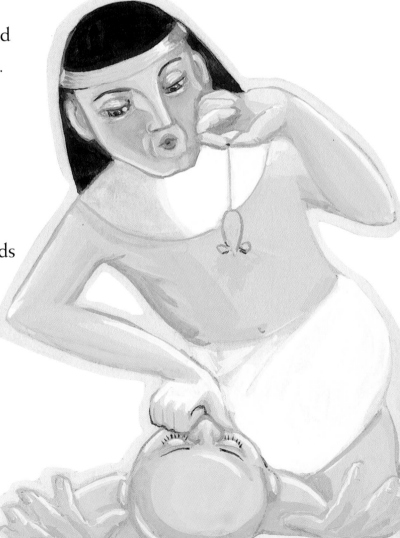

# TAXES

Today we have income tax,
Sales tax, and car tax.
Those taxes may seem like a curse.
But if you had lived in the
Days of old Egypt,
The taxes you paid were much worse.

It took lots of money
To build all those temples
And pay for the armies at war.
The pharaohs had lifestyles
Of sumptuous riches,
And yet they would always want more.

You didn't pay money, but
Part of your harvest.
Some farmers paid bushels of grain
Or jars of sweet honey
Or maybe fat cattle.
You paid, but you couldn't complain.

The taxmen kept records
Of infinite detail,
Assigning how much you would pay.
Those records tell stories
About ancient Egypt.
That's how we know so much today.

FOOD

Wealthy Egyptians ate ducklings and mutton.*
They liked being very well fed.
Their delicate pastries were flavored with honey,
While poor folks ate onions and bread.

Ancient Egyptians would eat with their fingers.
In those days it wasn't a crime.
Knives, forks, and spoons weren't used at the table
Till many years later in time.

*Mutton meat
Comes from a sheep.

CLEOPATRA

The fair Cleopatra was just seventeen
When she came to the throne and became Egypt's queen.

According to law, she was to rule with her brother,
But she and her brother kept fighting each other.
She needed strong allies. She found them in Rome.
They came with their armies to help her at home.

Clever and daring, she used her charms well.
Two great Roman leaders fell under her spell.
She threw lavish banquets, drank pearls in her wine,
And dressed as a goddess when guests came to dine.

Her influence grew, getting Rome all upset.
They thought Cleopatra was really a threat.
So they sent out a fleet and a battle ensued.
Cleopatra's brave sailors were quickly subdued.

When she saw that escape was out of her grasp,
She decided to die by the bite of an asp.
"I *will* not be captured and humbled," she said.
"I *will* not surrender, I'd rather be dead."

So she called in her servant, "Just one thing, I ask it.
Go bring me a snake, concealed in a basket."
She made her last plans and got carefully dressed,
Then reached for the snake, clutched it close
    to her breast.

The asp raised its head; its cruel fangs sank deep.
Cleopatra fell into a last, fatal sleep.

HE LIBRARY AT ALEXANDRIA

In ancient Alexandria,
Egypt's largest port,
Stood a famous library
With books of every sort.

Every manuscript and scroll
You'd ever want to read
Was right there in the library.
They met your every need.

You could learn about astronomy,
Medicine, biology,
Royal genealogy,
And even ichthyology.

Of course there were no books on tape,
No videos, no comics.
But you could read a lot of stuff
On ancient economics.

And you never had to worry
If your book were overdue.
With more than half a million books,
They'd never miss a few.

It had no children's section
(The one thing I'd protest),
But ancient Egypt's library
Was still the very best.

Genealogy (the study of your family or ancestors) is pronounced GEE-nee-AL-uh-gee. *Ichthyology* (the study of fish) is pronounced IK-thee-AL-uh-gee.

MORE ABOUT ANCIENT EGYPT

Books

Hart, George, Ed. *Ancient Egypt.* New York: Time Life, 1995.

McGraw, Eloise Jarvis. *The Golden Goblet.* New York: Puffin Books, 1990.

Shuter, Jane. *Egypt.* Austin, Tex.: Raintree/Steck-Vaughn, 1998.

Trumble, Kelly, and Laszlo Kubinyi (illustrator). *Cat Mummies.* New York: Clarion Books, 1996.

Websites

Egypt Fun Guide
http://www.seaworld.org/Egypt/egypt.html
Get lots of fun information about ancient Egypt from this Sea World website

Life in Ancient Egypt
http://www.clpgh.org/cmnh/exhibits/egypt/index.html
Learn about ancient Egypt from the Carnegie Museum of Natural History

Rosetta Stone and Ancient Egypt
http://www.clemusart.com/archive/pharaoh/rosetta/index.html
Learn about ancient Egypt from tour guide Rosetta Stone on this Cleveland Museum of Art website

Tale of Three Cities
http://www.nationalgeographic.com/3cities/
Find out how civilization has changed from Alexandria, Egypt, in A.D. 1 to Córdoba, Spain, in A.D. 1000 to New York City in A.D. 2000 on this National Geographic Society website

INDEX

ABOUT THE AUTHORS

Susan Altman and **Susan Lechner**, both graduates of Wellesley College, currently produce the Emmy Award–winning television program *It's Academic* in Washington, D.C., and Baltimore, Maryland. They have also produced *It's Elementary*, *Heads Up!*, and *Pick Up the Beat*. They are coauthors of *Followers of the North Star*, a book of rhymes for young people (also published by Children's Press). Ms. Altman is also the author of the play *Out of the Whirlwind* and the books *Extraordinary African-Americans* and *The Encyclopedia of African-American Heritage*.